ANIMALS AT WORK

HOW ANIMALS BUILD, DIG, FISH AND TRAP

WRITTEN BY ETTA KANER

ILLUSTRATED BY PAT STEPHENS

Kids Can Press

I'd like to thank Laurie Wark and Stacey Roderick for their editing expertise, superb organizational skills and pleasant personalities. Thank you also to Pat Stephens for her delightful, lifelike illustrations and to Marie Bartholomew for her fine design.

To Yael — EK

To Caitlin — PS

Kids Can Press acknowledges the financial support of the Ontario Arts Council, the Canada Council for the Arts and the Government of Canada, through the BPIDP, for our publishing activity.

Published in Canada by
Kids Can Press Ltd.
29 Birch Avenue
Toronto, ON M4V 1E2

Published in the U.S. by
Kids Can Press Ltd.
2250 Military Road
Tonawanda, NY 14150

www.kidscanpress.com

Edited by Laurie Wark and Stacey Roderick
Designed by Marie Bartholomew
Printed and bound in Hong Kong by Book Art Inc., Toronto

The hardcover edition of this book is smyth sewn casebound. The paperback edition of this book is limp sewn with a drawn-on cover.

CM 01 0 9 8 7 6 5 4 3 2 1
CM PA 01 0 9 8 7 6 5 4 3 2 1

Canadian Cataloguing in Publication Data

Kaner, Etta
     Animals at work : how animals build, dig, fish and trap

Includes index.
ISBN 1-55074-673-1 (bound)
ISBN 1-55074-675-8 (pbk.)

1. Animal behavior — Juvenile literature. I. Stephens, Pat. II. Title.

QL751.5.K36 2001   j591.5   C00-932962-5

Kids Can Press is a Nelvana company

Contents

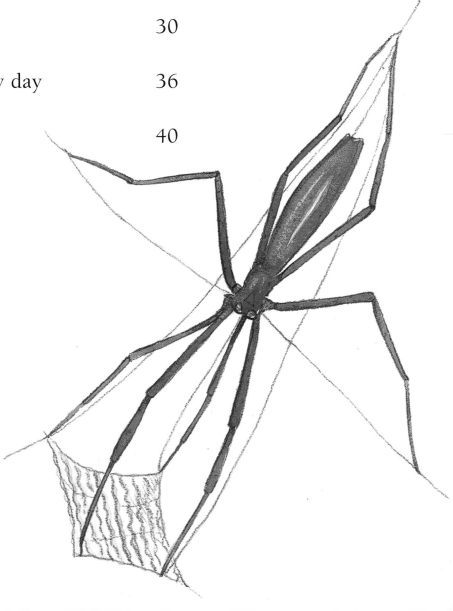

Introduction

If you were an animal, would you need to work? Definitely. You would need to work to stay alive. What kinds of work would you do? First of all, you'd work to get something to eat. You might build a trap out of silk, like a spider, or crack open eggs by throwing them against a rock, like a mongoose. In addition to working for your food, you'd work to build a home. If you were a termite, you would build a tower as tall as a house with tiny chewed-up bits of wood. If you were a swiftlet, you'd build a nest out of spit. You would also have to work hard to attract a mate and protect your children.

In this book, you will find out about how animals work to survive. You will learn about the structures that animals build and the unusual materials they use to construct them. Did you know that alligators build giant incubators out of rotten plants? Or that some fish protect their eggs with bubbles? This book has lots of activities and experiments that will help you understand how and why animals work. Find out what it would be like to build like a bee, fish like a heron, store food like a mole, drink like a chimp and much more.

Green-backed heron

Home sweet home

Like you, animals live in a home. For an animal, a home can be a safe place to sleep, raise babies or store food. A home can also protect an animal from bad weather and enemies. Many animals work hard to build their homes.

How do animals know what to do? Scientists say that animals build by instinct. This means that they are born knowing just what to do. Honeybees use instinct to build amazing hives. But not all honeybees are builders. Only the females work. They are called worker honeybees.

If you were a honeybee ...

- you would be a female.
- you would work with thousands of other honeybees to build wax walls inside your hive. You would get the wax from a tiny slit in your belly.
- you would shape the wax with your jaws to form six-sided rooms, or cells. There are hundreds of these cells on each wall or honeycomb.

Honeybee

Getting into shape

Homes come in all kinds of shapes. Rabbits and moles live in homes that are long and narrow. Many birds build nests that are round like a soup bowl. Some caterpillars have homes shaped like a tent. Each animal builds a home that is shaped for its needs.

A dome home

Hold the ends of an egg between the palms of your hands. Now press as hard as you can. It's impossible to break it, right? That's because each end of the egg is a dome, which is a very strong shape. No wonder a soldier crab builds its shelter in the shape of a dome.

The soldier crab stays in its shelter while the tide is in. The shelter protects it from drowning. A soldier crab works hard to build its home.

1. The soldier crab digs a shallow pit in the sand.

2. It runs backward in a circle, pushing up sand to make a low wall.

3. The crab continues to run until the wall gets higher and higher and finally curves in.

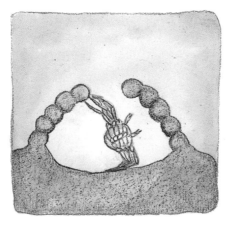

4. It fills in the hole at the top with a tiny ball of sand.

5. Finally, it makes the top thicker by pushing up more sand from the bottom.

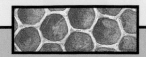

Honeybee cells

The rooms or cells in a honeybee's home are in the shape of a hexagon (six-sided). Why don't honeybees use other shapes? Try this experiment to find out.

1. Use the lid to trace circles on paper, making sure they touch each other. Do you see the space in between the circles? If beehive cells were round, there would be a lot of wasted space in the hive.

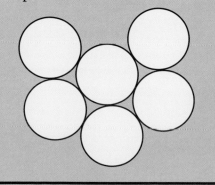

2. Look at the hexagon shapes in the beehive on page 7. The walls touch on all sides. This pattern saves space and allows bees to use wax for two cells at a time. If the cells were circles, bees would need more wax for the parts that don't touch.

3. To find out why bees don't use triangle or square cells, measure the distance around the three shapes on the right. Each shape has the same area, or space, inside. Start at one corner and lay the wire along the sides until you come back to the starting point. Make sharp corners. Make a mark on the wire. Straighten the wire and lay it along the ruler to see how long it is.

4. After you've measured all three shapes, you should find that the hexagon has the shortest perimeter, or distance around. It needs the least amount of wax to build. By building their cells out of hexagons, bees need to work less.

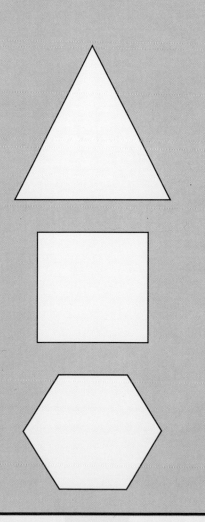

Digging in

Some animals build their homes by digging. They might dig under the ground, into snow or even into the bottom of the sea. Badgers are expert ground diggers. With its strong claws, a badger can dig faster than you can dig with a shovel. Still, it might take a badger a while to dig its burrow. That's because a burrow may have as many as 20 rooms connected by long tunnels. Many of these rooms are lined with moss, ferns and leaves. This lining makes a soft bed for a badger.

Badger

Yellowhead jawfish

Can you guess from its name what the yellowhead jawfish uses to dig its home? Its huge jaws! First, the jawfish scoops out sand from the sea bottom to make a deep hole. Then it presses shells and pieces of coral into the top part of the hole to form a tunnel. During the day, the tunnel entrance is open in case the jawfish needs to make a fast getaway. At night, the jawfish closes the opening with a large stone to keep out predators.

Dig a well

Jawfish are often called well diggers because their homes look like the wells that people build. Both jawfish and people line the sides of the holes that they dig. Try this experiment to find out why.

You'll need:

a trowel

a place to dig

about 20 large gravel stones

1. Dig a hole in the ground about 15 cm (6 in.) wide and 15 cm (6 in.) deep.

2. Try to make the sides of the hole straight up and down. What problems do you have?

3. Press the stones into the sides of the hole, while holding the dirt in place with your hand.

The stones should help to stop the dirt from caving in. They are like the shells and coral that the jawfish uses to line its tunnel.

Showing off

Animals do many amazing things to attract a mate. Usually, it's the male that works hard to attract a female. Male ghost crabs build a sand pyramid outside their burrows to help females locate them. Three-spined stickleback fish glue together bits of water plants to form a tunnel nest for females. And some birds, like the one on this page, even build and decorate a stage for dancing.

Satin bowerbird

If you were a male satin bowerbird ...

- you would build a stage out of grass and twigs to attract a female.
- you would decorate the stage with blue objects — flowers, berries, feathers, and even yarn or glass beads that you might find.
- you would dance on the stage, picking up objects with your beak to show a female visitor.

13

The singers and ...

Spring is here and birds are singing. Male birds sing to attract a mate and to tell other males to stay away. But birds aren't the only animals that sing to attract mates. Can you match the clues with the pictures of these singing animals?

Frog

Humpback whale

Grasshopper mouse

1. I am very small.
My song sounds like chirping.
I stand on my hind legs when I sing.

2. I live in water.
When I sing, my throat puffs out like a balloon.
Sometimes my song sounds like a croak.

3. I have a big mouth.
My singing sounds like honking.
When a female gets close, I honk faster so that she'll pay attention to me and not to other males.

4. I live in water.
My song can be heard hundreds of miles away.
I sing for hours at a time.

Answers on page 40

Hammerhead bat

... the dancers

Some male birds attract females by dancing. They dance on a special stage that they work hard to build.

The male lyrebird doesn't just build one stage. It builds ten or more. The male builds round stages in the forest by stamping down plants, digging out roots and kicking up earth. Once a stage is built, it's show time. The lyrebird holds his fancy feathers over his head and turns round and round. At the same time, he sings a loud song. The stagemaker clears the forest floor so carefully that it looks like someone swept it with a huge broom. On his stage, he lays huge leaves with their pale undersides showing. When a female comes along, the stagemaker dances around with first one leaf and then another leaf in its mouth.

Lyrebird

Stagemaker

When the male bird of paradise builds a stage, he cuts off the branches above it. This lets the sunlight shine on him when he does his dance. And what a dance it is! He stretches up his neck and hops from side to side. Then he nods his head so quickly that the six long feathers on his forehead are a blur.

Bird of paradise

15

Giving gifts

Another way a male animal works to attract a female is to give her a gift. Often, the gift is food. Many male spiders catch insects for a present, which they gift wrap in silk.

Sometimes it's easier for an animal to steal food than to catch it. That's what some male hanging flies do when they want to give a gift of food to a female. The male fly lands beside another male who is holding food in his mouth and acts like a female hanging fly. When the male with the food moves closer, the thief grabs the food and flies away.

Hanging flies

But food isn't the only kind of gift that a male animal can give a female. In Central America, the giant damselfly's present is a puddle of water. Why would a female want a puddle of water? To lay her eggs in. And getting a puddle of water is harder than you might think. Because there aren't many around, males will fight over a puddle, and the winner claims it for his own.

Giant damselfly

Some people say that the best gifts are the ones you make. But making a gift takes time. The male weaverbird spends weeks building a nest to attract a female. He uses long strips of grass to weave his nest. He also makes many kinds of loops and knots. But he doesn't tie the knots very tight — just in case he might have to undo them. If he can't find a female who likes his nest, the male takes the nest apart and starts all over again.

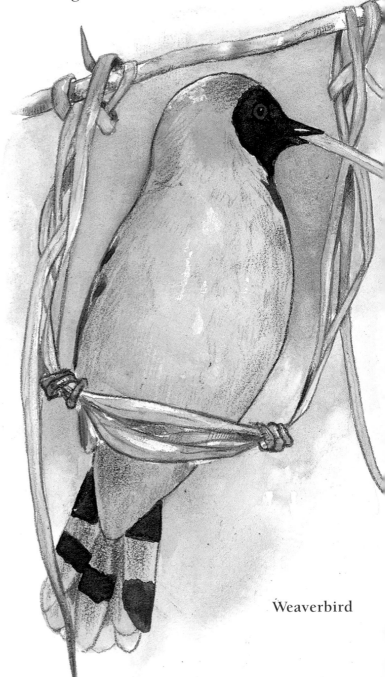

Weaverbird

All in knots

Can you tie an overhand knot or a half hitch? Or how about a running knot? Weaverbirds use these knots when they build their nests. People use them when they camp, sail, climb, fish or tie packages and shoelaces. What's unbelievable is that the weaverbird ties these knots with its beak and feet. You can use your hands to do the same. All you need is a piece of rope.

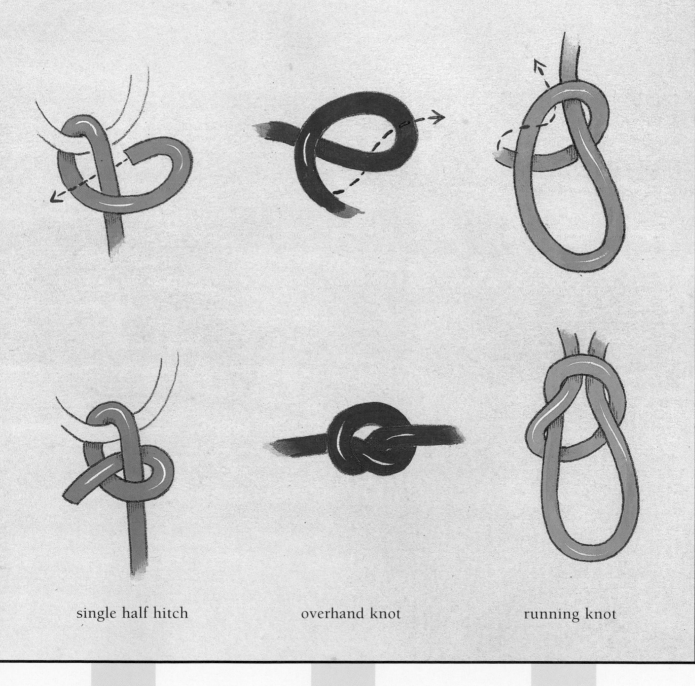

single half hitch   overhand knot   running knot

Safe and sound

When animals lay eggs, they lay them in a safe place. This is a place where enemies won't eat them. It's also a place where the eggs won't be too hot or too cold, too wet or too dry. Once the eggs hatch, the young have to be safe there, too. How do animal parents make such a place? Some animals, like the Smith frog, use mud to build a wall around the eggs and young. Others build nests. Still others carry their eggs and young with them to make sure they are safe.

If you were a female nursery web spider ...

- you would carry your eggs in a silk sac wherever you went. The sac would be so big that you would have to walk on tiptoe.
- you would carry your egg sac in your jaws.
- you would build a nest out of leaves tied together with silk. When the young were ready to hatch, you would hang your egg sac in the nest.

Nursery web spider

Blowing bubbles

Some animals use bubbles to protect their young. They make bubbles that look like soap foam. The foam makes the eggs or young inside invisible to an enemy.

The male paradise fish builds a nest by blowing air bubbles near the surface of the water. When this foamy nest is finished, the female lays her eggs in the water. The eggs float up into the nest. If any eggs miss the nest, the male catches them in his mouth and spits them into the nest.

Gray tree frogs make bubble nests with their feet. Males and females get together in a group to make a nest high up in a tree. To start, the females produce a sticky liquid. Then, all the frogs kick at the liquid with their strong hind legs. The kicking pushes air into the liquid just like egg beaters do when you beat egg whites. In fact, the nest looks like a large ball of beaten egg whites. The females lay their eggs inside the nest and, in a few days, they hatch into tadpoles.

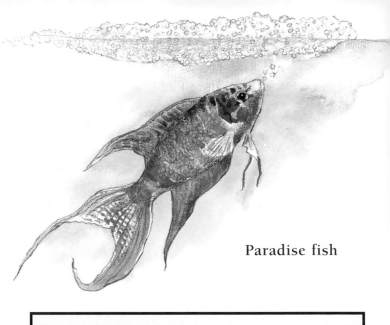

Paradise fish

Rising eggs

Why do the eggs of the paradise fish float up to the surface of the water? To find out, put a spoonful of cooking oil in a glass. Pour some water into the glass. The oil is lighter than the water, so it floats to the top. Inside each egg of the paradise fish is a small glob of oil. The oil makes the tiny egg float to the top of the water.

Gray tree frogs

It looks like spit

The next time you see white foam on a plant stem, take a closer look. That foam is not someone's spit. It is the home of a spittlebug. The spittlebug is the nymph (young) of the froghopper insect. It covers its body with bubbles to hide itself from hungry predators. To make the bubbles, the spittlebug makes a pool of liquid from the plant juices that it eats. Then it blows air into the juices to form a foam that lasts a week or longer. How can the bubbles last so long? Try this to find out.

You'll need:

a drinking straw

half a glass of water

liquid detergent

1. Put the straw into the glass of water and blow bubbles. How long do the bubbles last?

2. Put a squirt of detergent into the water. Mix it with the straw.

3. Blow bubbles with the straw. Which bubbles lasted longer?

The soap keeps the bubbles strong so that they don't burst right away. The liquid of the spittlebug is like the soapy water. It stops the bubbles from bursting.

Heating up

How do animals hatch their eggs? They keep them warm. Most birds keep their eggs warm by sitting on them. But not the mallee fowl. It builds a giant compost heap for the job. The male and female dig a deep hole in the ground and fill it with layers of leaves and sand. As the leaves rot, the pile heats up. The male checks the temperature by sticking his bill into the mound. After about four months, when the temperature is just right, the female lays her eggs. More layers of leaves and sand are piled on top, and the male keeps checking the temperature until the eggs hatch.

Brush turkeys also build a compost heap to keep their eggs warm. The male builds it out of wet leaves and soil. He checks the temperature of the mound every day. If the pile is too hot, he pokes holes in it. If the pile isn't hot enough, he adds more wet leaves to it.

Female mallee fowl

Birds aren't the only animals that build mounds to keep their eggs warm. The American alligator does it, too. But in this case, the female does all the work. With her sharp teeth, she bites off branches and plants. She carries them in her mouth to the edge of the water, where she makes a large pile. At the top of the pile, she lays her eggs. Then she covers the eggs up with more plants. As the plants rot, the pile heats up. To help this process, the alligator splashes water on the pile with her tail. When the young are beginning to hatch, their mother hears them and opens up the mound.

The inside story

Do you have a composter for garden and food waste? Believe it or not, it can get as hot as 66° C (151° F) inside a composter. This happens when the millions of tiny organisms or bugs that live there chew up the leaves and food scraps that you put into it. To keep them active, just add water and stir.

Male mallee fowl

Catch that meal

What do you do when you're hungry? You probably open your fridge or cupboard—and there's your food! It's not that easy for animals. Animals have to catch their food before they can eat it. Some animals build traps and wait nearby for their prey to be caught. Other animals fish for their food with bait. And some, like the fish on this page, use unusual tools to catch their dinner.

Archer fish

If you were an archer fish ...

- you would eat insects.
- you would have a groove on the roof of your mouth. When you pressed your tongue against the groove, you would make a tube. This tube would be like a water gun—perfect for shooting water droplets.
- you would shoot water droplets at insects on nearby plants. The drops would knock the insects into the water, where you would gobble them up.
- you would have perfect aim up to a distance of 150 cm (5 ft.).

Practice makes perfect

An archer fish can only hit its target with lots of practice. That's because when it looks at an insect above the water, the insect is not really where it seems to be. How does this happen? Try this to find out.

You'll need:

a drinking straw

water

a glass jar or pitcher with straight sides

1. Pour water into the jar so that it is half full.

2. Put the straw in the water.

3. Crouch down and look up at the surface of the water in the jar. Does the straw look bent?

It seems to bend in a direction opposite to where the straw really is above the surface. When light goes from water to air or from air to water, it bends. This is called refraction. Refraction makes the straw look bent. Refraction also makes it hard for an archer fish to know where the insect really is. That's why it needs practice to have perfect aim.

Going fishing

People aren't the only ones who go fishing. Animals go fishing, too. Like us, most animals use bait. But their bait is often very unusual.

Green-backed heron

The green-backed heron uses a feather, berry or dead insect for bait. The heron throws its bait onto the surface of the water. When a fish comes to investigate the bait, the heron grabs it with its long, thin bill. Poor fish, but lucky heron!

Before an assassin bug goes "fishing" for termites, it must catch its bait. Oddly enough, its bait is a dead termite. The assassin bug catches its bait at the entrance to a termite nest. After it sucks the juices out of the termite's body, it's ready to fish. It dangles the termite's body at the opening of the nest. When the other termites see it, they come running to investigate — right into the assassin bug's mouth.

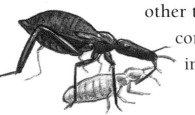

Assassin bug

The Temminck's snapper turtle uses its tongue for bait. It lies on the bottom of a lake with its mouth wide open and the red tip of its tongue wiggling. The tip looks like a tasty worm to a passing fish.

Temminck's snapper turtle

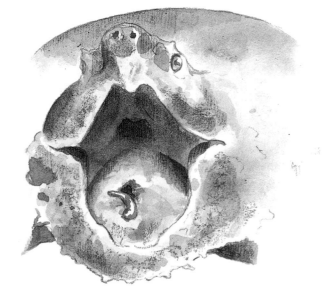

It's a trap!

Some animals build traps to catch food. The traps on these pages are made out of silk. Here are some clues to help you identify them.

1. The bolas spider catches moths by swinging around a single strand or line of silk. Moths get stuck in a sticky ball of silk at the end of the swinging strand.

2. The ogre-faced spider holds its net-like trap with its front legs. When an insect comes along, the spider stretches the net wider and throws it over the insect.

3. The triangle spider builds a triangular web between two twigs. It holds a thread attached to one corner of the triangle. As soon as an insect brushes against the web, the spider alternately tightens and loosens the thread until the insect is tangled up in the web.

4. The larva (young) of the caddis fly builds an underwater trap. Its net is shaped like a funnel. Flowing water carries tiny animals into the net for the larva to eat.

5. The purseweb spider lives inside its trap, which looks like a long, slender silk tube. The tube may lay on the ground or even go up the side of a tree. When an insect crawls onto the tube, the spider bites it through the silk and pulls it inside.

Answers on page 40

A.

B.

D.

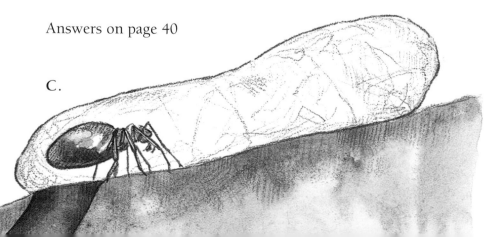

C.

Staying unstuck

This garden spider builds a round silk web to trap insects. When insects fly into the sticky web, they get stuck. Why doesn't the spider get stuck, too? Flies get stuck on the sticky circular threads. The threads that look like the spokes of a wheel are dry. That's where the spider travels.

E.

Get ready to eat!

Even if an animal has found food, it can't always dig right in. The animal might have to break open a hard shell to get at the tasty food inside. It might have to get the food out of a hard-to-reach place. Or it might even clean its food before eating it.

If you were an otter ...

- you would eat clams, crabs, mussels and lobsters.
- you would break their shells by banging them many times on a flat stone. You would lay the stone on your chest while you floated on your back.
- you would carry your favorite stone in your armpit as you looked for more food on the ocean floor.

Using tools

If you wanted to eat a clam or a crab, you might use a hammer or a nutcracker to break through its hard shell. These are both simple tools. Spoons, forks and knives are other simple tools. People use them every day to prepare food. Some animals also use tools to get their food ready to eat. Chimpanzees are champs at this.

Chimpanzees make special probe-sticks to get at their favorite food—termites. A chimp uses its strong fingers to make small holes in a termite nest.

Then it looks for a twig. If the twig is too long, it breaks off a piece. If the twig is too rough, it removes leaves and tiny stems. Once it has a perfect probe, the chimp pushes it into the termite nest. When the chimp gently pulls out the stick, it is covered in termites. The chimp simply wipes the stick across its mouth for a delicious meal.

Strange but true

How do some kinds of ants carry berry juice back to their nest? They hold bits of wood, leaf or mud in the juice until it is soaked up. Then the ants carry the "sponge" back to their nest.

Chimpanzee

Soaking it up

When a thirsty chimpanzee looks for water, it might find a small pool in the fork of a tree. But how does it get the water out? First, the chimp crumples up a bunch of leaves by chewing on them. Then it dips the leaves into the water. The leaves soak up the water like a sponge. By sucking on the leaves, the chimpanzee has a refreshing drink. Why does the chimpanzee crumple up the leaves before dipping them into the water? To find out, try this.

You'll need:

a large container of water

2 identical glasses

6 large green leaves

a sponge

1. Hold 3 of the leaves together under the water for 30 seconds.

2. Take out the leaves and let most of the water drip off.

3. Squeeze the water out of the leaves into a glass.

4. Crumple the other three leaves with your fingers. Hold them in a loose ball under the water for 30 seconds.

5. Squeeze the water out of the ball into the other glass.

Which set of leaves absorbed more water? When you crush the leaves, you create many little pockets or spaces of air. Water fills up the spaces of air. You can see this happen when you hold a sponge under water. If you squeeze it, air bubbles escape from the tiny pockets in the sponge as water fills them.

Food at last!

Do you have to work as hard as these animals before you get to eat your dinner?

When crows want to eat shellfish or eggs, they break the shells open by dropping them on a rocky surface.

When an ocelot catches a bird, it plucks out the feathers before eating it. Each time it gets a mouthful of feathers, it shakes its head from side to side to remove the feathers from its mouth.

Leaf-cutter ants grow fungus for their food. They chew up bits of leaves, add manure and wait for the fungus to grow. When it's ripe, the ants break off little balls of fungus to eat

Cleaner wrasse eat parasites that grow on the skin of larger fish. One wrasse might clean as many as fifty large fish in one hour. Now that's a lot of work!

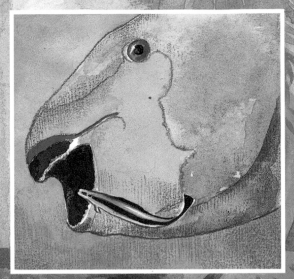

An agouti eats only roots that have been peeled. Holding a root in its paws, an agouti tears off strips with its huge front teeth until its food is clean.

To break open an egg, a spotted skunk kicks the egg against a hard surface with its hind leg.

Saving for a hungry day

Just as you save leftovers for the next day, animals save food when there is more than they can eat. Some animals even hoard, or store, food for winter, a time when food is scarce. They store their food in all kinds of places: in trees, in holes in the ground, in tunnels, in fence posts or even behind walls. This is harder than you may think. Animals must first build a storage place and then they must use a lot of time and energy gathering food for it.

If you were a male pika ...

- you would be related to rabbits and hares.
- you would collect long grasses in the summer and fall to eat in the winter. You might travel several hundred feet from home to gather your food.
- you would put the grasses into piles to dry into hay.
- you would build a stone wall around the grass piles. The wall would protect the grass from the wind.

Hoarders

Since a mole doesn't hibernate, it needs to collect lots of food to get through the winter. Most of that food is earthworms. A mole can store more than 1000 earthworms in one storage space. How does it keep so many earthworms fresh? It bites off their heads. The earthworms are still alive, but they can't wriggle away.

Acorn woodpeckers work in groups to collect and store acorns for the winter. They drill thousands of holes in a dead tree or even a fence post. Each hole is filled with an acorn. When winter comes, they just fly to their larder (food cupboard) and chomp away.

Strange but true

Some honeypot ants are used like jars to store extra nectar in their abdomens. They are called repletes. When other honeypot ants are hungry, they rub the repletes until they bring up some drops of nectar from their abdomens.

When a leopard kills a big animal like an antelope, it can't eat it all in one sitting. It also can't leave it on the ground for later. Other animals might help themselves to the leftovers. So the leopard drags its kill high up in a tree. There, the leopard can eat its meal in peace. It can also leave what it doesn't eat and not worry about uninvited guests. After all, who's going to climb that high for a meal?

One food that the American red squirrel hoards is mushrooms. Before the squirrel stores the mushrooms in a tree stump, it spreads them out on a branch to dry. This stops the mushrooms from rotting. In the winter, the squirrel has a supply of dried mushrooms to eat.

Index

Answers

Page 14
1. Grasshopper mouse
2. Frog
3. Hammerhead bat
4. Humpback whale

Pages 28–29
1. D
2. A
3. E
4. B
5. C